by Anne C. Hallowell
Barbara G. Hallowell

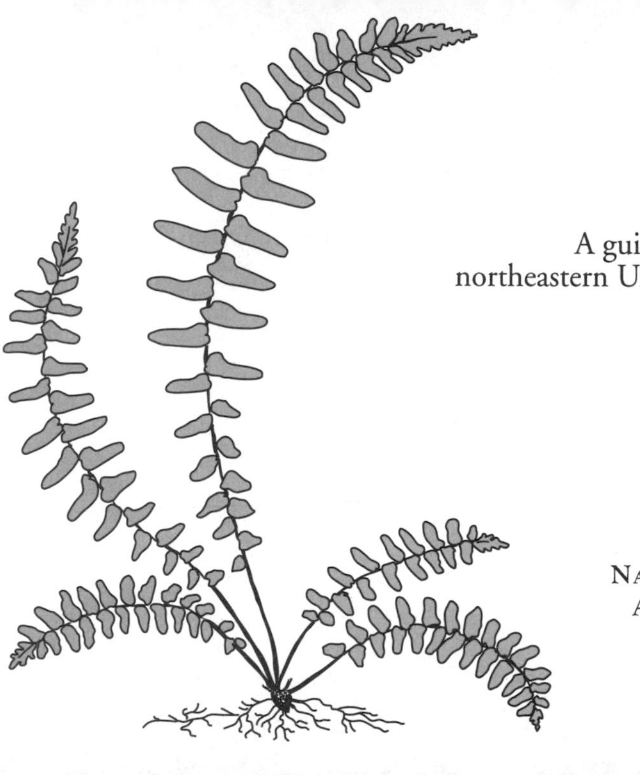

# Fern Finder

A guide to native ferns of central and northeastern United States and eastern Canada

Second Edition

by Anne C. Hallowell
and Barbara G. Hallowell

illustrations by Anne C. Hallowell

NATURE STUDY GUILD PUBLISHERS
A division of Keen Communications
Birmingham, Alabama
keencommunication.com

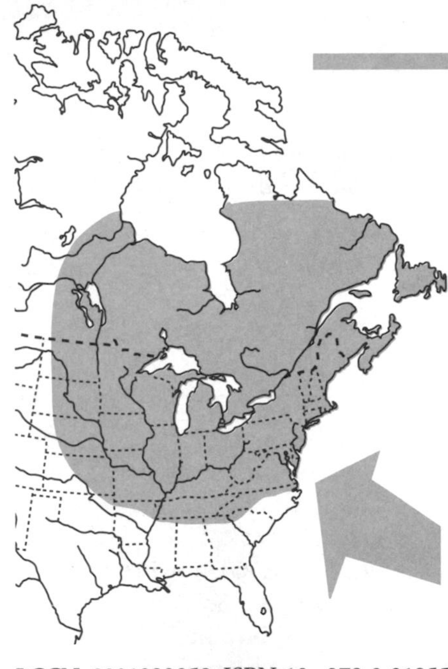

## How to use this book

- See pages 1-7 for information that may help you use the identification key.
- Select some typical fronds from the fern you wish to identify, and turn to page 8.
- Make the first choice, either  or   and proceed.
- Consider all choices under each symbol. Use a hand lens to see tiny fern parts.

When you've made the final choice, arriving at the name of your fern, compare your frond with the illustration and check the other features shown.

Several ferns are included twice because of variations in the way they look.

This book is for ferns that grow naturally in this area.

LCCN: 2001090352 ISBN-13: 978-0-912550-24-4 ISBN-10: 0-912550-24-4

## Parts of a fern



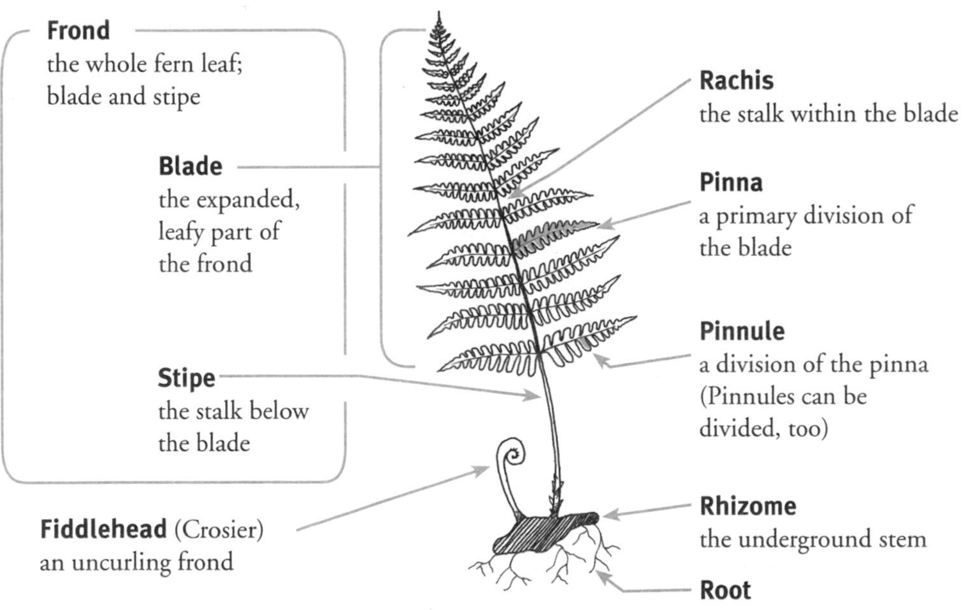

## ② To identify a fern, look at:

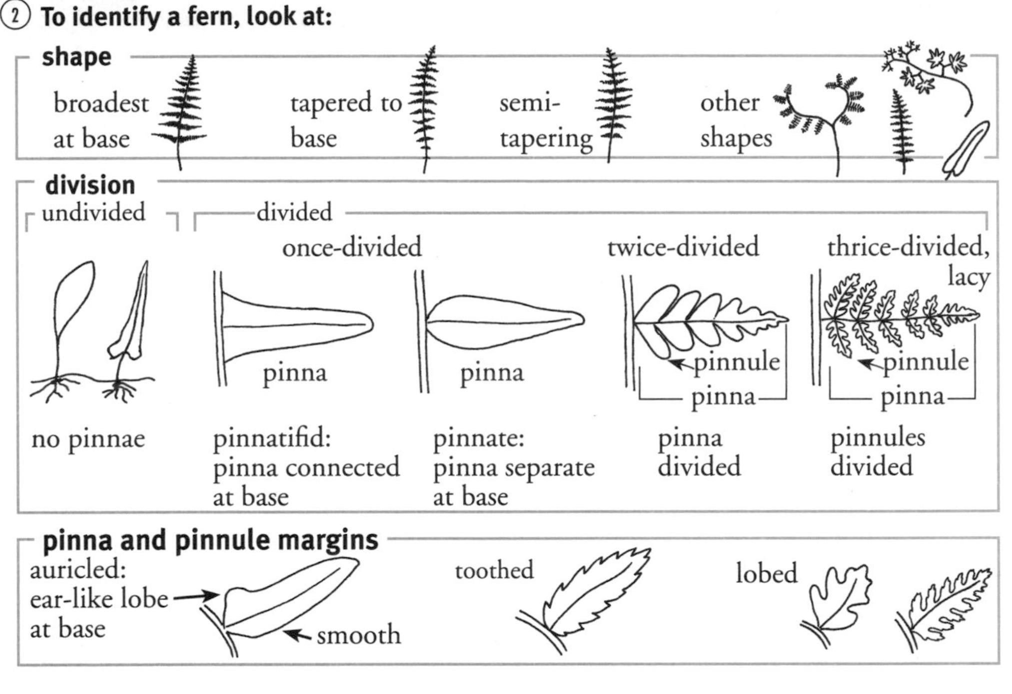

## growth form

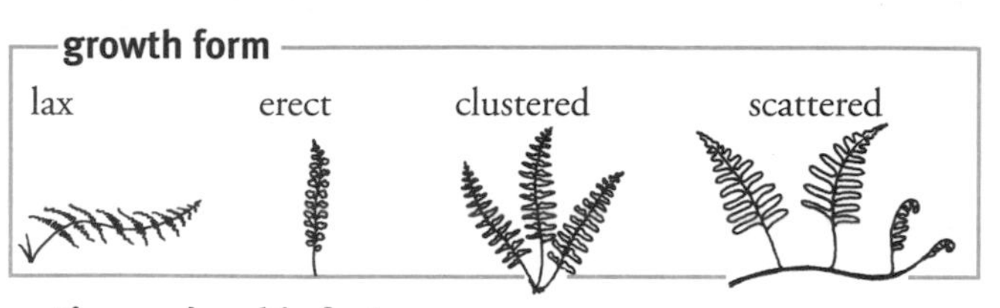


## stipe and rachis features

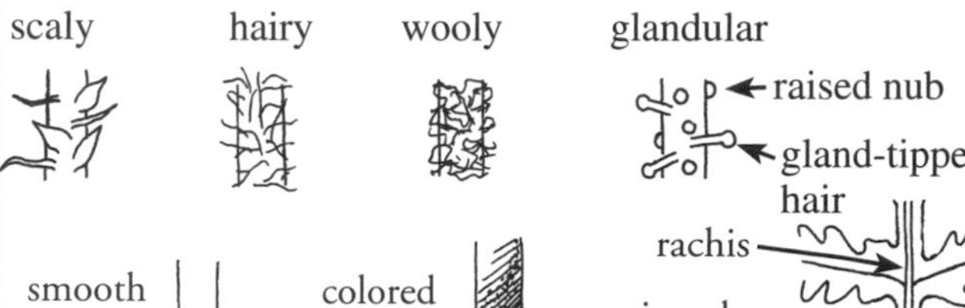


## other features

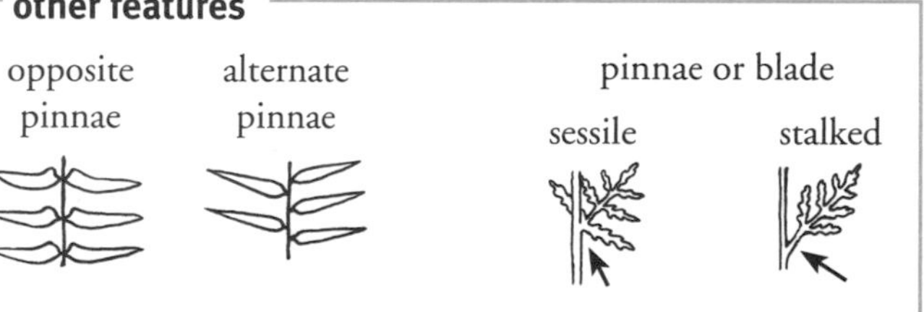


## reproductive features

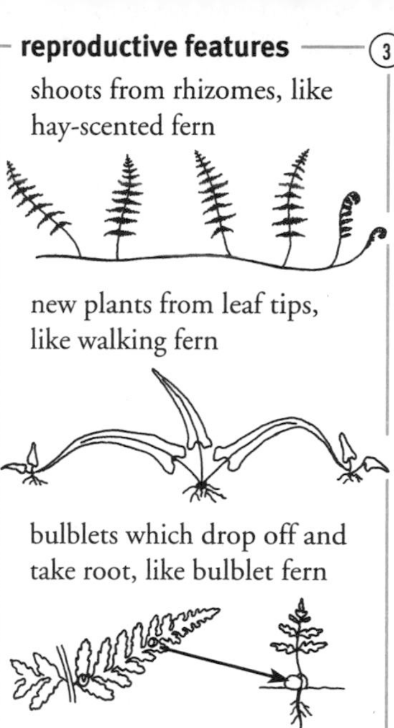


spore-bearing parts—see next page (important)

(4) Ferns produce nearly microscopic reproductive cells called **spores**.

Spores develop inside spore cases called **sporangia**.

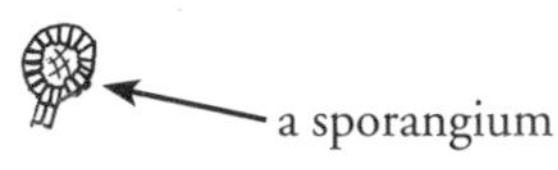


A fern frond with sporangia is a **fertile frond**.

A fern frond without sporangia is a **sterile frond**.

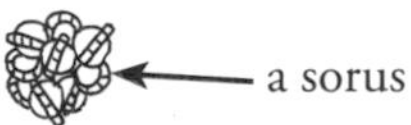


Sporangia are usually grouped into clusters called **sori** (singular sorus) or fruit dots on the backs of the blades.

Each fern species has a typical sorus shape and arrangement.

**examples of sorus shapes**

round 

elongate 

curved 

**examples of sorus arrangements**

marginal

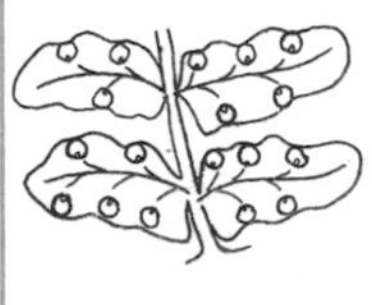

oblique

lined along margins

along midvein

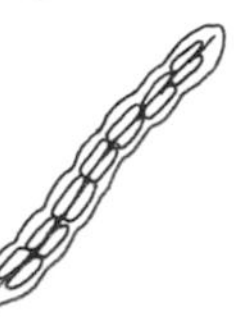

scattered

A thin layer of cells, an **indusium**, usually covers the sorus while the spores are developing inside the sporangia.

**examples of indusium shapes**

- kidney-shaped, attached at one side — as in wood ferns
- round, attached centrally — as in Christmas fern
- star-shaped, attached under sorus — as in woodsias
- elongate, attached at one side — as in chain ferns
- curved, attached at one side — as in lady fern
- cup-like — as in hay-scented fern
- no indusium — as in polypody

As spores ripen, the indusium pulls back, shrivels, and often disappears, exposing the sporangia. When spores are fully ripe, the sporangia burst open and spores spill out.

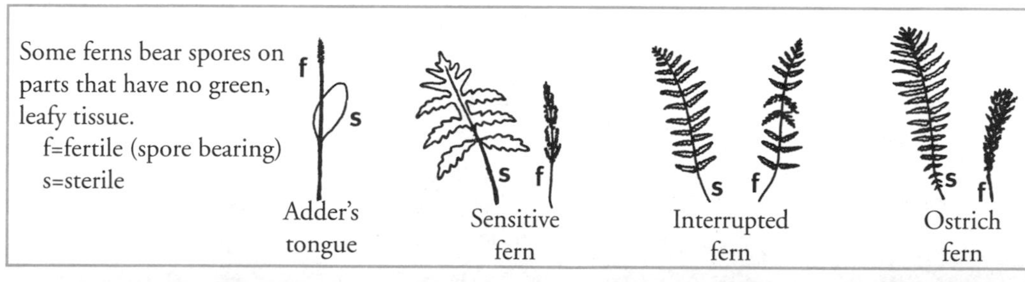


Some ferns bear spores on parts that have no green, leafy tissue.
f=fertile (spore bearing)
s=sterile

## 6 The life cycle of a fern

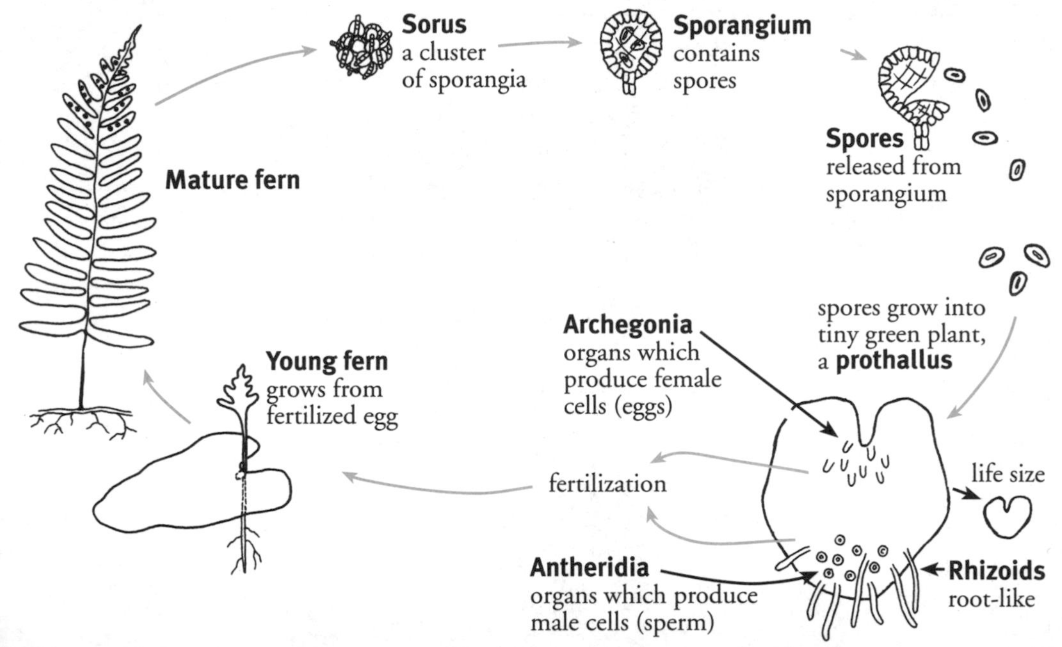

**Symbols show the habitat in which you are likely to find each fern growing.**

**woods**—in mostly shaded places

**fields**—in open, weedy fields or grassy meadows

**rocks**—among or on rocks, cliffs, walls, or ledges

**wet areas**—in bogs and swamps, often "with feet wet"

**moist banks**—along banks of streams and edges of wet areas, not "with feet wet"

**trees**—on tree trunks and large, spreading limbs

---

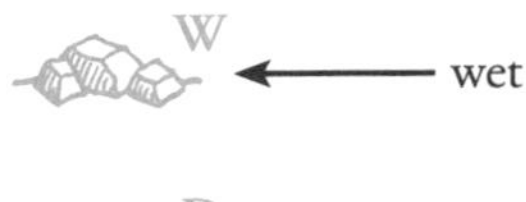


wet

dry

Many ferns grow in more than one habitat. For example, a fern which grows in woods and on moist banks has the symbol

## Begin here

If blade (the green, leafy part of the frond) is divided, go to this symbol

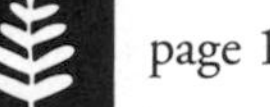

page 11

If blade is not divided, go to this symbol

below

If blade is grass-like, wiry, and curly, it is **Curly Grass Fern**
*Schizaea pusilla*

If blade is leaf-like, go to

next page

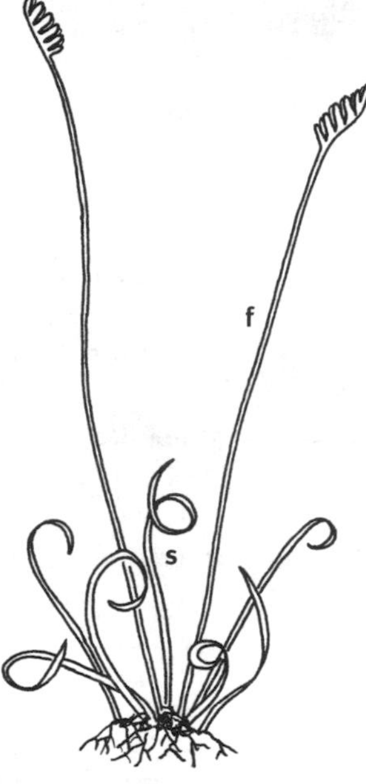

1-5 in
2.5-12.5cm

If blade is oval or elliptical with a fertile stalk arising from its base, go to 

If blade has heart-shaped base and elongate sori on underside, go to 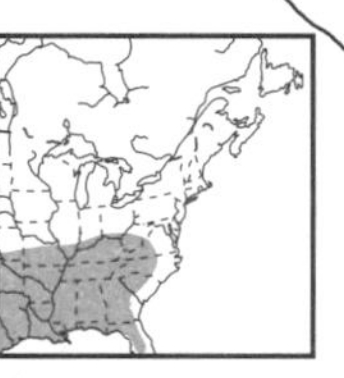 next page

W

3-8 in

7.5-20cm

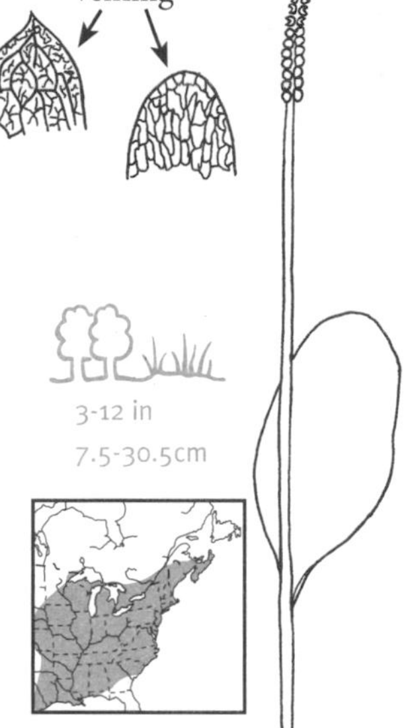

If blade tip has a tiny, sharp point, it is **Limestone Adder's-Tongue** *Ophioglossum engelmannii*

If tip is blunt, it is **Adder's-Tongue** *O. vulgatum (O. pycnosticum)*

from 9

If blade is narrow with a long, pointed tip that arches to the ground to form new plants, and sori are scattered, it is **Walking Fern**

*Asplenium rhizophyllum*
*(Camptosorus rhizophyllus)*

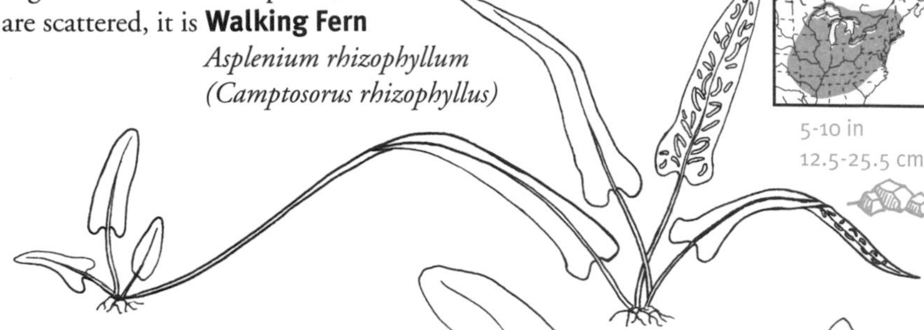

5-10 in
12.5-25.5 cm

7-14 in
17.5-35.5 cm

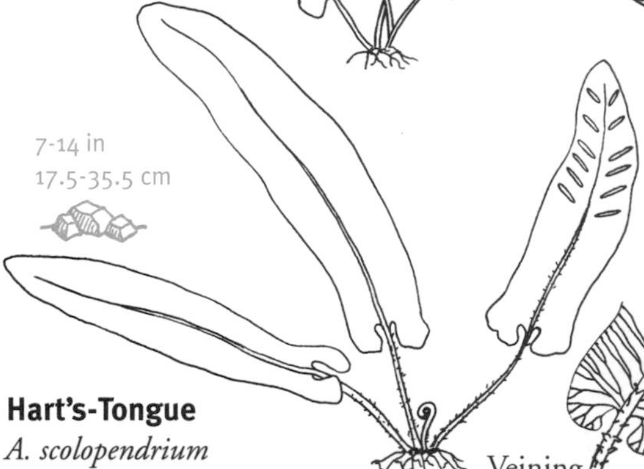

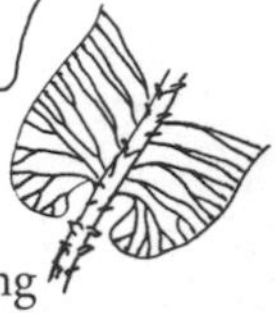

If blade is strap-like with a blunt tip and oblique sori, it is **Hart's-Tongue**

*A. scolopendrium*
*(Phyllitis scolopendrium)*

Veining

If blade is vine-like, and each pinna divides into two hand-shaped parts, it is **Climbing Fern**
*Lygodium palmatum*

from 8

If blade resembles a four-leaf clover it is
**Water Clover**
*Marsilea* spp.

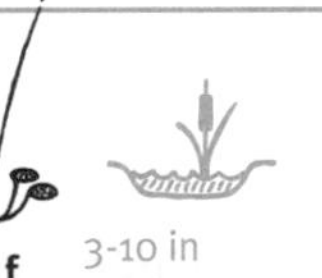


If blades have scale-like pinnae and the plant is free-floating on water, it is
**Mosquito Fern**
*Azolla* spp.

If none of the above, go to

next page

from 11

If blade is once-divided, like this:  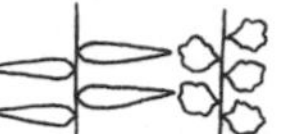 go to 

If it's more than once-divided, like this:  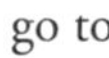 go to  page 22

If stipe is succulent, and sporangia are clustered toward the tip of a fertile stalk that branches from the stipe, go to 

If stipe is firm and sporangia are on the backs of pinnae or are on a separate fertile stalk, go to  page 14

If pinnae are rounded or fan-shaped, go to  next page

If they're elongate and lobed, go to  next page

If pinnae are broadly fan-shaped, it is **Moonwort** *Botrychium lunaria*

If they're mostly rounded, it is **Little Grape Fern** *B. simplex*

If blade is a broad triangle and is sessile, it is **Lance-leaved Grape Fern** *B. lanceolatum*

If blade is a narrow triangle with a short stalk, it is **Daisy-leaved Grape Fern** *B. matricariifolium*

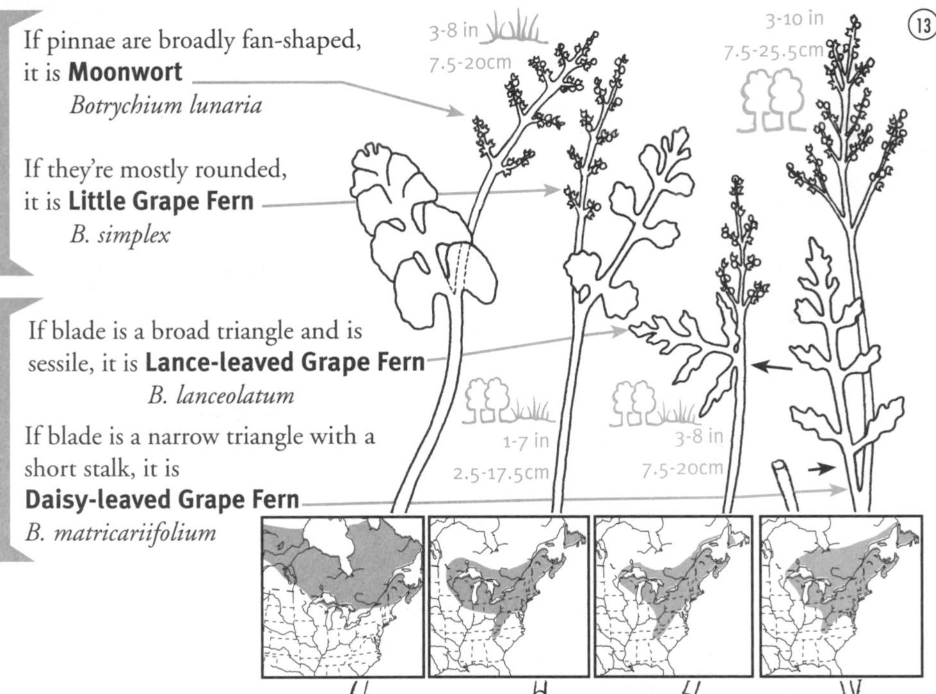

from 12

If blade is pinnatifid, like this:
Note: in a few species the lower one or two pairs of pinnae may be pinnate.

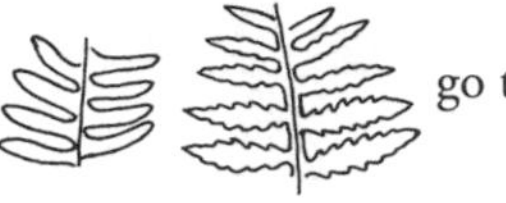

go to 

If blade is pinnate, like this:

go to  page 18

If frond is less than 3 inches (7.5cm) wide, go to  p. 16

If frond is more than 5 inches (12.5cm) wide and sporangia are:

on backs of pinnae, go to  p. 34

on separate fertile stalks, go to →  next page

If most pinnae are nearly opposite, and sori are in bead-like cases on a separate fertile stalk, it is

**Sensitive Fern**

*Onoclea sensibilis*

If most pinnae are alternate, and sori are elongate in broken, chain-like rows on narrow fertile pinnae, it is

**Netted Chain Fern**

*Woodwardia areolata*

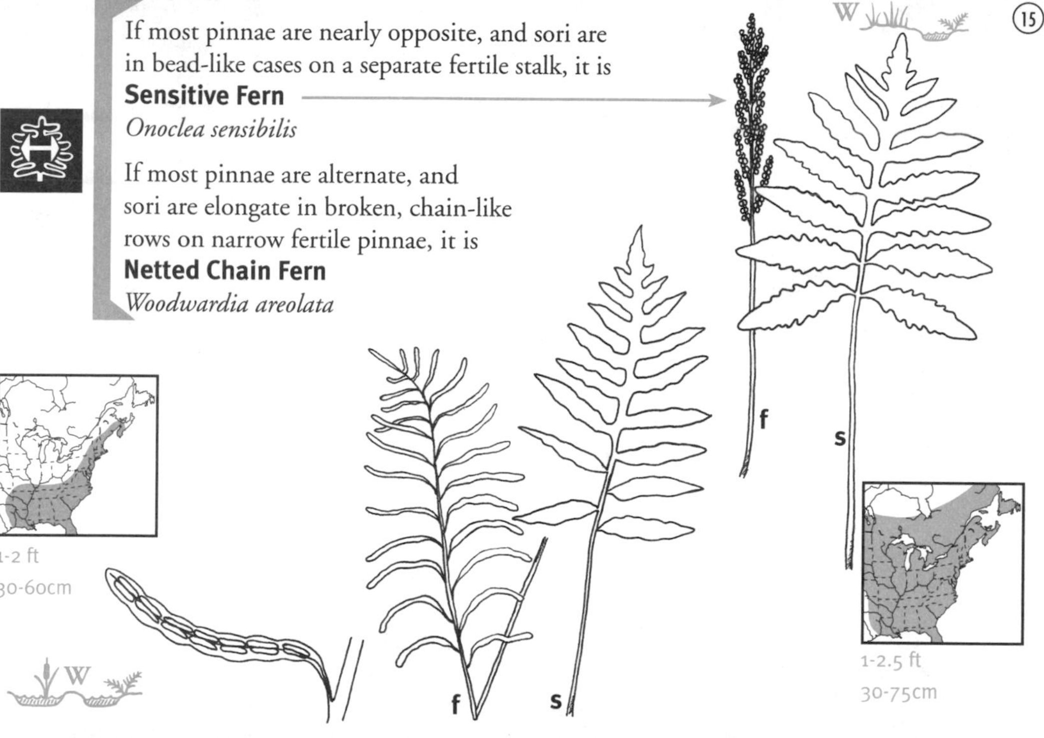

from 14

If blade is oblong and deeply cut almost to the tip, and sori are round, go to

If blade is long, narrow, and tapers to a thin point, its upper third not deeply cut, and sori are elongate, go to  next page

3-10 in
7.5-25.5cm

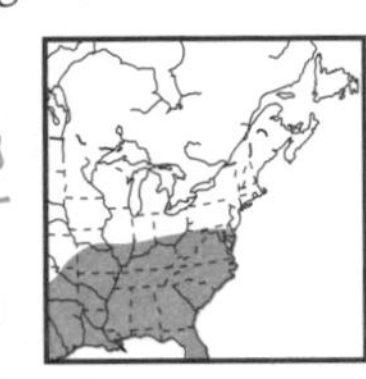

4-15 in
10-38cm

If back of blade looks pock-marked with small dark-centered scales, and fronds curl and appear dead when dry, it is **Resurrection Fern**
*Pleopeltis polypodioides*
*(Polypodium polypodioides)*

If back of blade is without scales, it is **Common Polypody**
*Polypodium virginianum*

dried frond

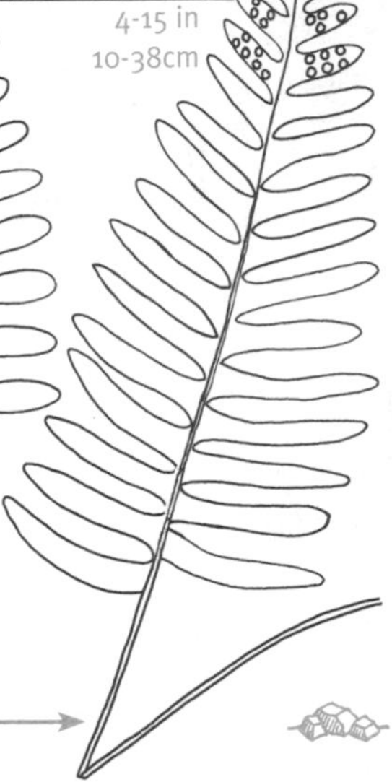

If pinnae are irregular in shape, and stipe and lower rachis are dark, it is **Scott's Spleenwort**
*Asplenium ebenoides*

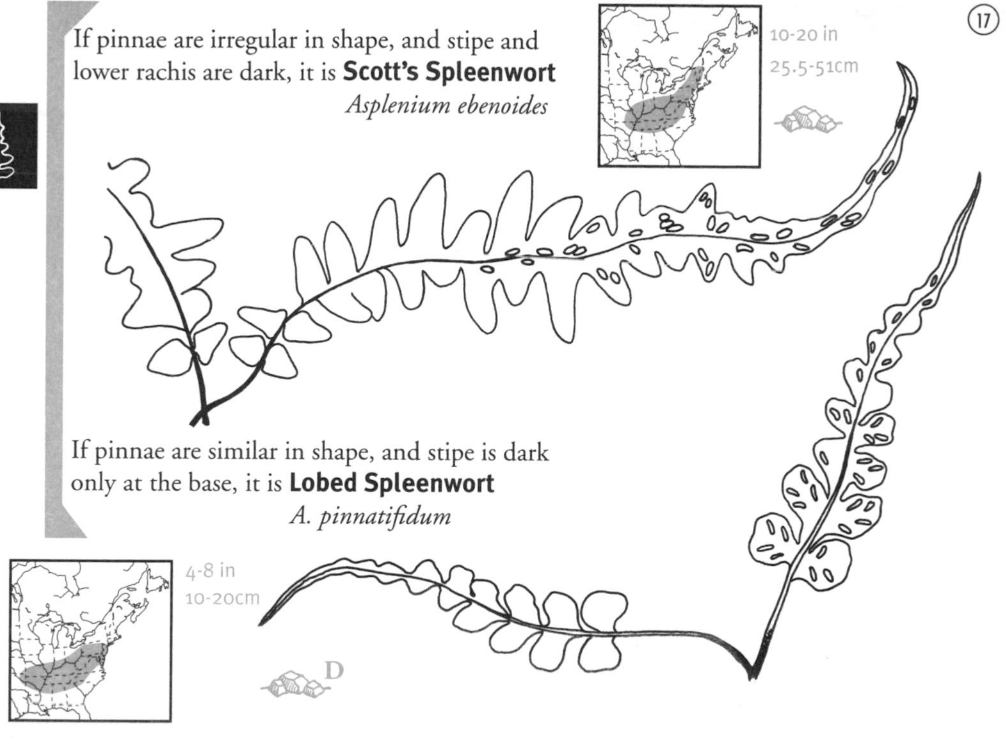


If pinnae are similar in shape, and stipe is dark only at the base, it is **Lobed Spleenwort**
*A. pinnatifidum*

from 14

If stipe and rachis are heavily scaled, and indusia are round and attached centrally, go to

If stipe and rachis are scaleless or very sparsely scaled, and indusia are elongate, go to

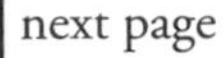

next page

If blade tapers to a point at the base and sterile and fertile pinnae are similar, it is **Northern Holly Fern** *Polystichum lonchitis*

If blade is semi-tapering, and upper pinnae of fertile frond are abruptly narrower and shorter than lower pinnae, it is **Christmas Fern** *P. acrostichoides*

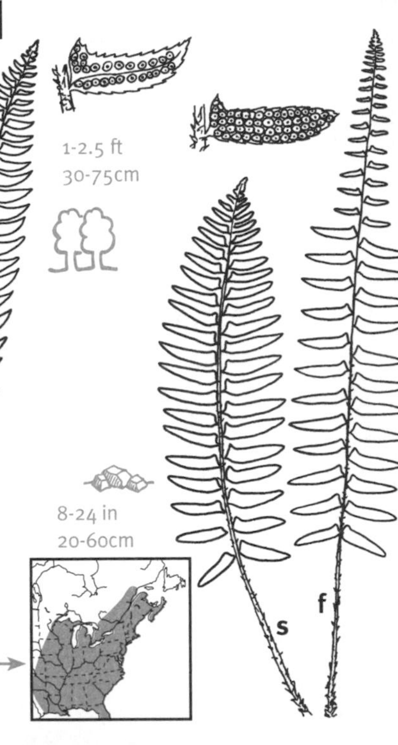

If pinnae have smooth margins and sharply pointed tips, and blade is wider than 4 inches (10cm), it is **Glade Fern**

*Diplazium pycnocarpon*
*(Athyrium pycnocarpon)*

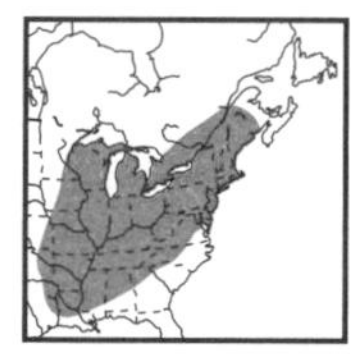

1-4 ft
30-120cm

If pinnae are toothed or slightly lobed and blade is less than 2 inches (5cm) wide, go to

next page

from 19

If pinnae are elongate and auricled, go to  next page

If pinnae are nearly round with a wedge-shaped base, go to 

3-7 in
7.5-17.5cm

If rachis is green and delicate, it is **Green Spleenwort**
*Asplenium trichomanes-ramosum*
*(A. viride)*

4-8 in
10-20cm

If rachis is dark and wiry, it is **Maidenhair Spleenwort**
*A. trichomanes*

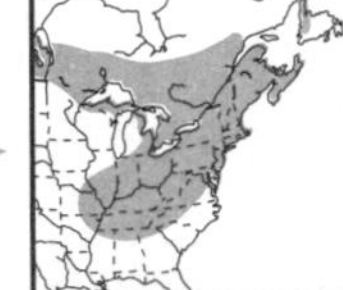

If upper third or half of rachis is green, it is **Bradley's Spleenwort**
*Asplenium bradleyi*

If rachis is all black to purple-brown, or green only toward the tip, go to

If pinnae are alternate, and fertile fronds stand erect above the smaller, spreading, sterile fronds, it is **Ebony Spleenwort**
*A. platyneuron*

If pinnae are opposite, and fertile and sterile fronds are similar and stand erect, it is **Black-stemmed Spleenwort**
*A. resiliens*

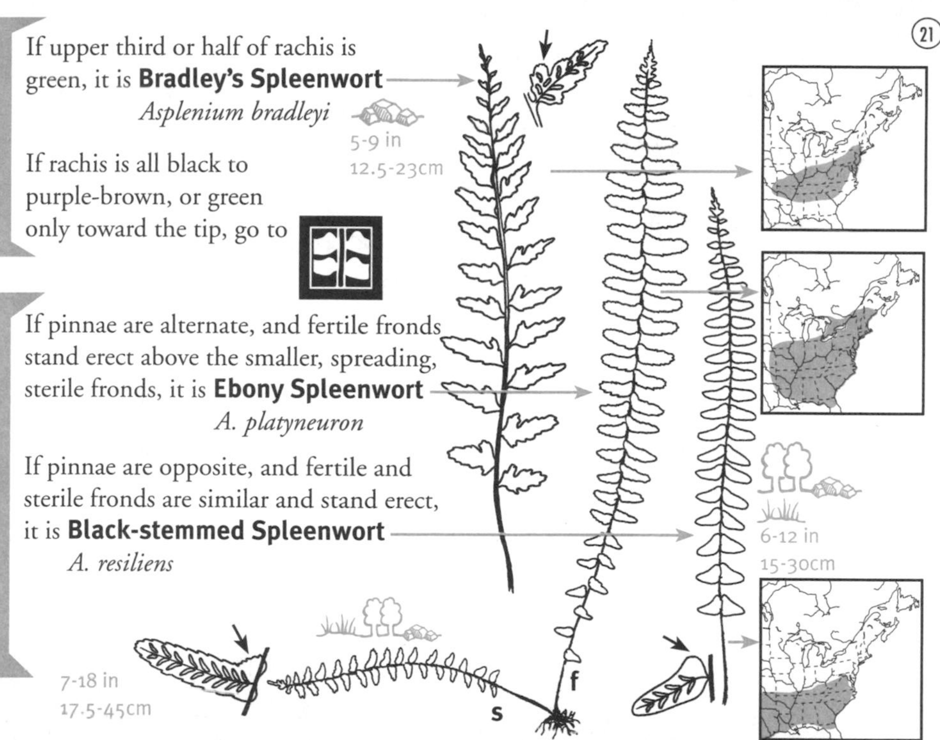

from 12

If both stipe and rachis are black to dark brown and wiry (look carefully—hairs can obscure this) and sori are along curled margins, go to 

If frond lacks this combination of characteristics, go to  page 28

If pinnules and sori look like this: 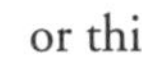 or this: 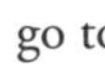 go to  next page

If they look like this:  or this: 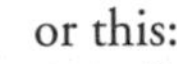  go to  page 24

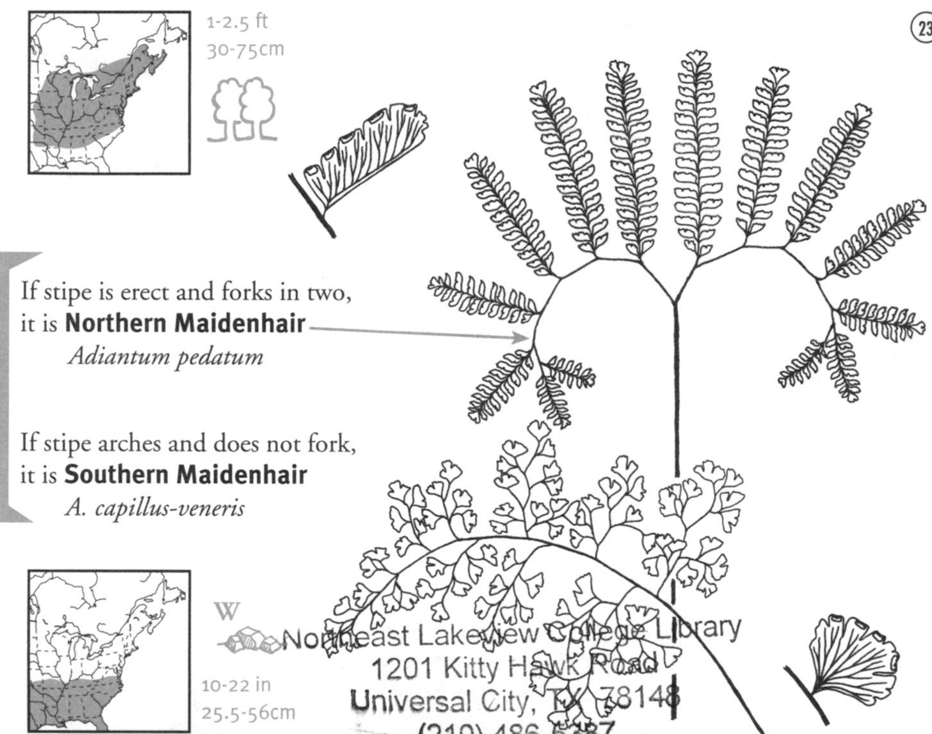


If stipe is erect and forks in two, it is **Northern Maidenhair**
*Adiantum pedatum*

If stipe arches and does not fork, it is **Southern Maidenhair**
*A. capillus-veneris*

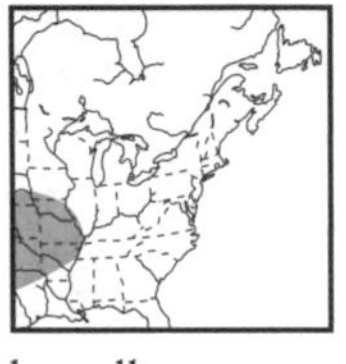

If blade is white-waxy beneath and broadly triangular, it is **Powdery Cloak Fern**
*Argyrochosma dealbata*

from 22

If it lacks white wax beneath and is oblong, go to  

If marginal line of sori is continuous, like this:  or  go to  next page

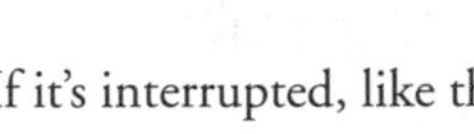

If it's interrupted, like this:  go to  page 26

If pinnules are lobed or auricled,
it is **Alabama Lip Fern**
*Cheilanthes alabamensis*

If not, go to

If stipe and rachis are hairy,
it is **Purple Cliffbrake**
*Pellaea atropurpurea*

If they're hairless and shiny,
it is **Smooth Cliffbrake**
*P. glabella*

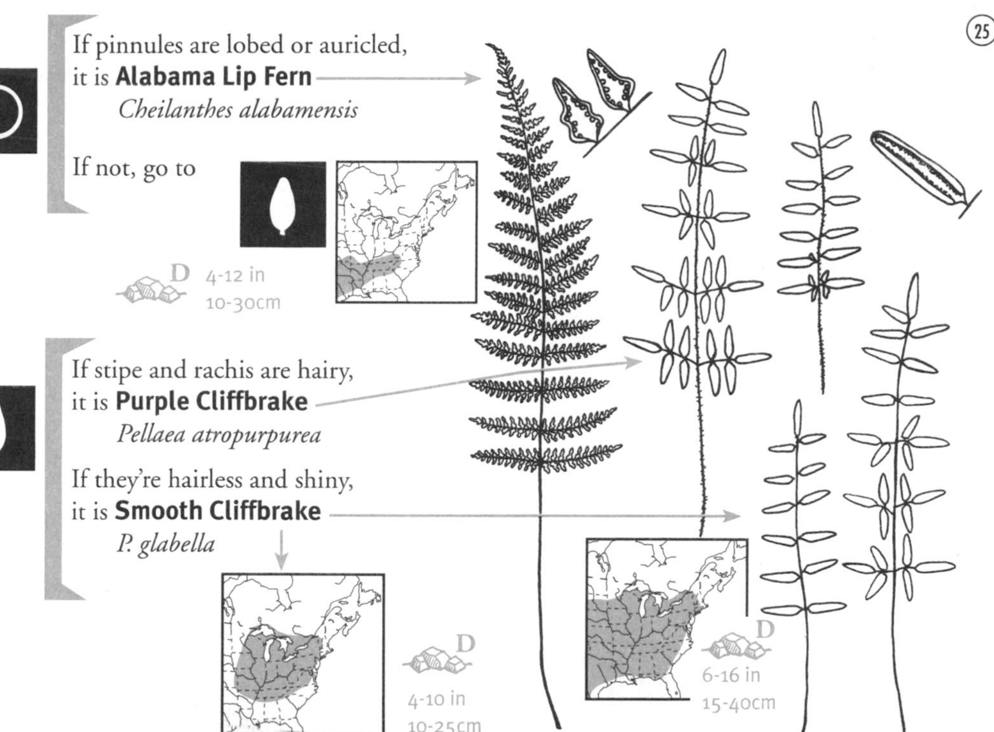

from 24

If stipe and rachis have narrow, light-colored scales and hairs, and blade is densely woolly and beady, it is **Woolly Lip Fern**

*Cheilanthes tomentosa*

If stipe and rachis have hairs but lack scales, go to next page

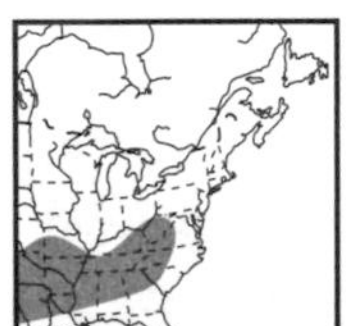

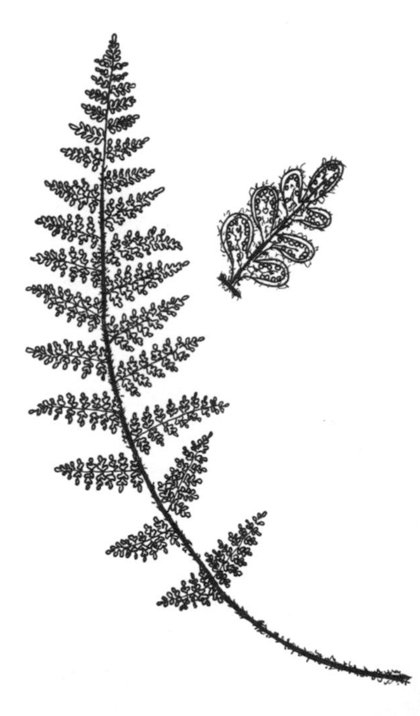

If blade is densely hairy underneath but sparsely hairy above, and fronds are densely clustered, it is **Slender Lip Fern**

*Cheilanthes feei*

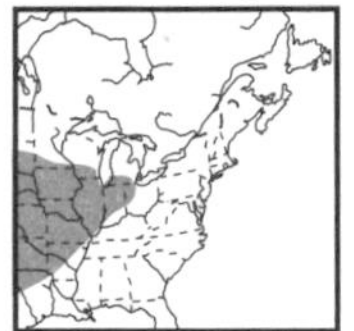

D

2-6 in
5-15cm

If blade is densely hairy both underneath and above, and fronds are loosely clustered, it is **Hairy Lip Fern**

*C. lanosa*

D

4-12 in
10-30.5cm

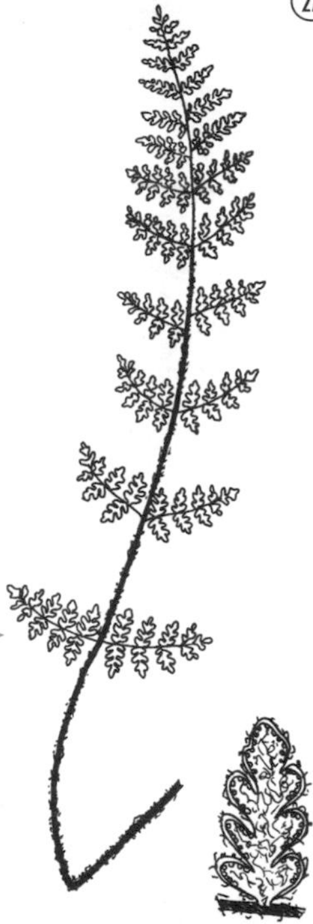

from 22

If blade is clearly broadest at the base, like this:   go to  next page

If blade is long-tapering, diminishing almost to a point at the base, like this:  go to  page 38

If blade shape is not clearly either of the above, go to  page 40

If stipe is succulent, and sporangia are clustered toward the tip of a fertile stalk that branches from the stipe, go to  next page

If stipe is firm, and sori are on the backs of the pinnae, go to 

If blade branches into three parts, like this:  go to  page 32

If not, go to  page 34

from 29

If fertile stalk arises at base of blade, like this:

go to

next page

If fertile stalk arises further down, it is one of four species of grape ferns with confusing intergrading forms that make identification difficult.

**Blunt-lobed Grape Fern**
*Botrychium oneidense*

**Dissected Grape Fern**
*B. dissectum*

**Leathery Grape Fern**
*B. multifidum*

**Sparse-lobed Grape Fern**
*B. biternatum*

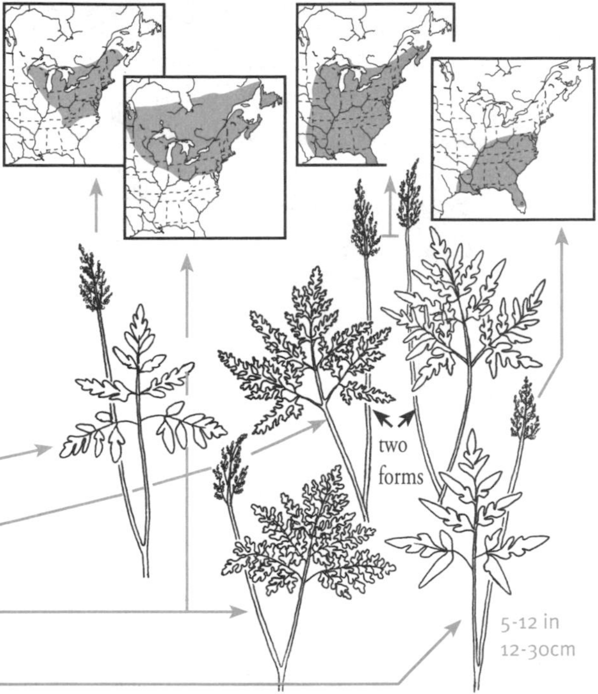

two forms

5-12 in
12-30cm

If blade is a narrow triangle,
it is **Daisy-leaved Grape Fern**
*Botrychium matricariifolium*

If it's a broad triangle,
go to ▲

▲

If blade is lacy and 3-10 inches (7.5-25.5cm) long,
it is **Rattlesnake Fern**
*B. virginianum*

If it's not lacy and is shorter,
it is **Lance-leaved Grape Fern**
*B. lanceolatum*

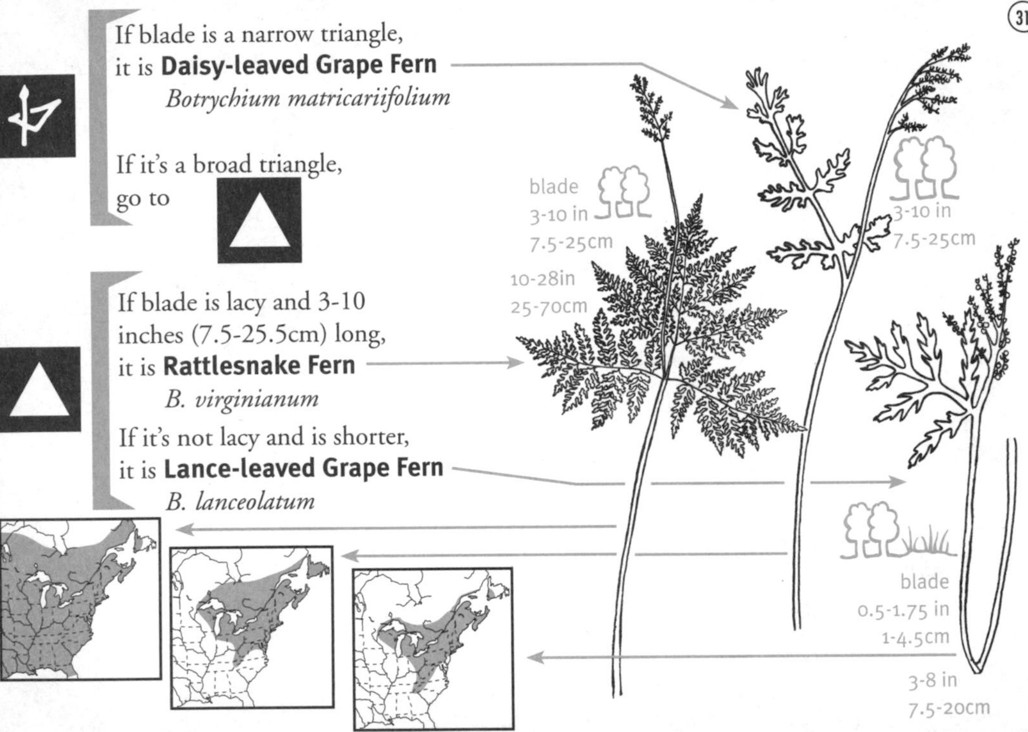

32

from 29

If frond is coarse, tough, 1-5 feet (3O-150cm) tall, and has sori in lines along curled margins,
it is **Bracken**
*Pteridium aquilinum*

If frond is delicate,
6-18 inches (15-45cm) tall,
and has round sori, go to

If blade is lacy it is **Mountain Fragile Fern**
*Cystopteris montana*

If not, go to next page

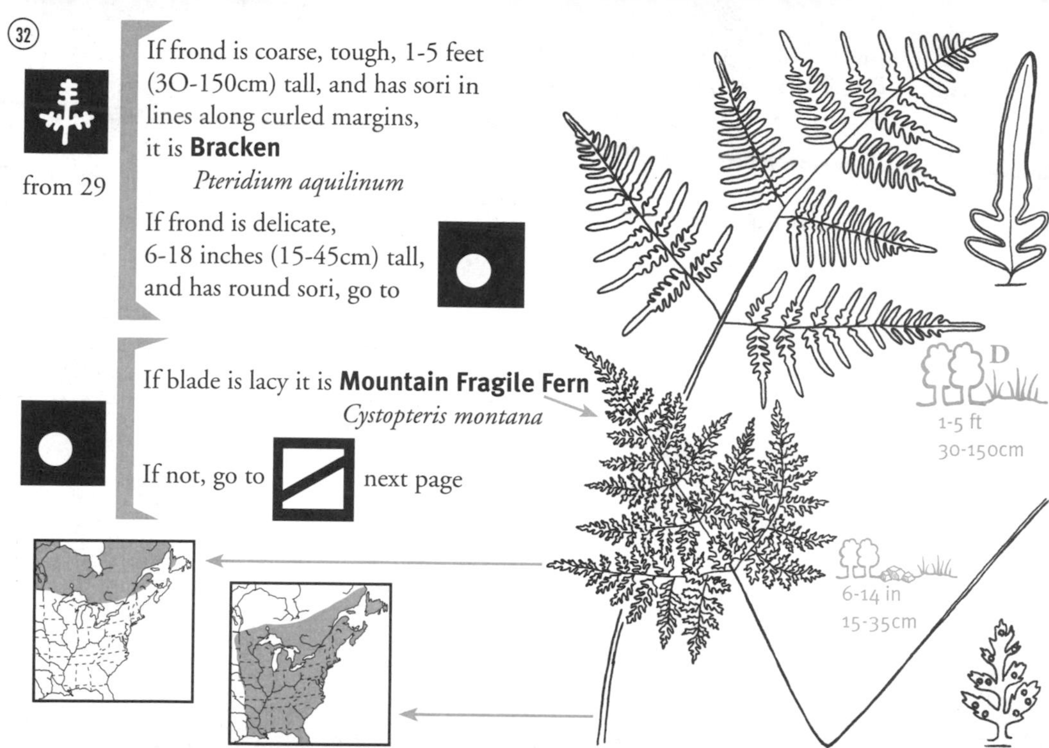

If frond is densely glandular and aromatic, and basal pinnae are smaller than whole upper portion of blade, it is **Limestone Oak Fern**
*Gymnocarpium robertianum*

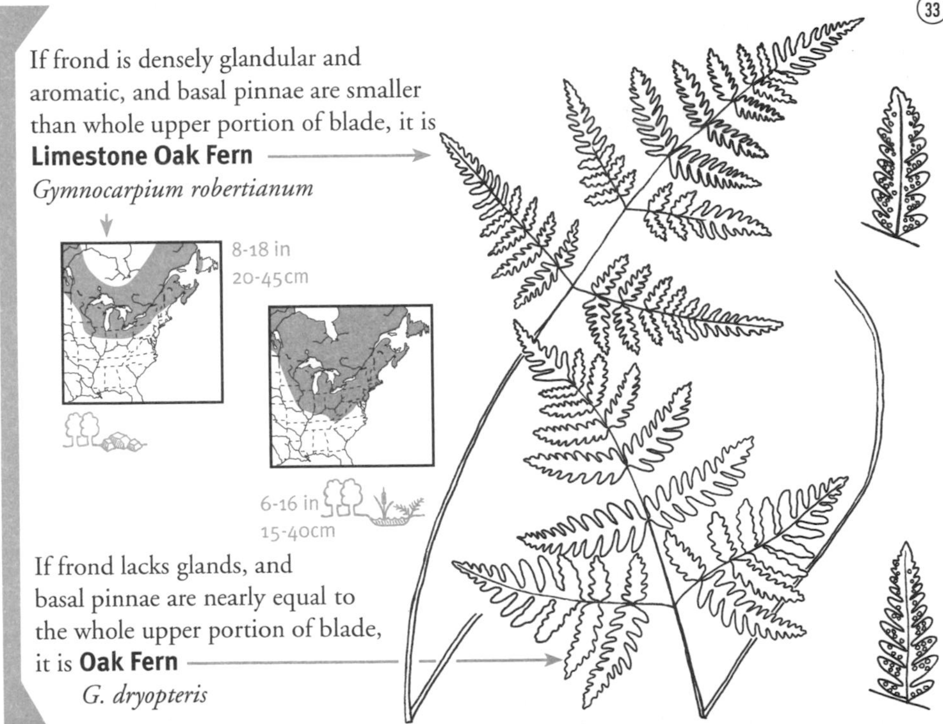


If frond lacks glands, and basal pinnae are nearly equal to the whole upper portion of blade, it is **Oak Fern**
*G. dryopteris*

34

from 29

If rachis is winged, like this: go to 

wing

If not, go to  next page

from 14/ above

If lowest pinnae are longest and winged at the rachis, and most blades are broader than long, it is **Broad Beech Fern**

*Phegopteris hexagonoptera*
*(Thelypteris hexagonoptera)*

If lowest pinnae are not longest and not winged at rachis, and most blades are longer than wide, it is **Narrow Beech Fern**
*P. connectilis (T. phegopteris)*

8-18 in
20-45cm

1-2.5 ft
30-75cm

If stipe is much shorter than rachis, and frond is a lax, long triangle, often with bulblets scattered on its back side, it is **Bulblet Fern**

*Cystopteris bulbifera*

1-3.5 ft
30-105cm

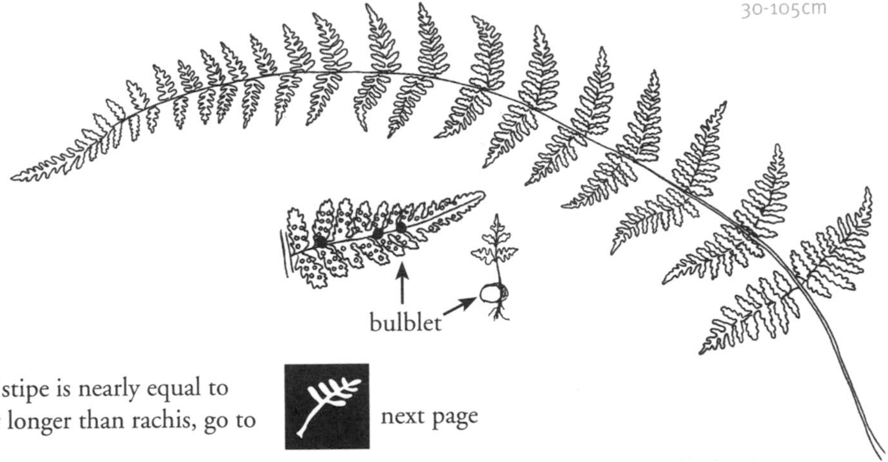

bulblet

If stipe is nearly equal to or longer than rachis, go to next page

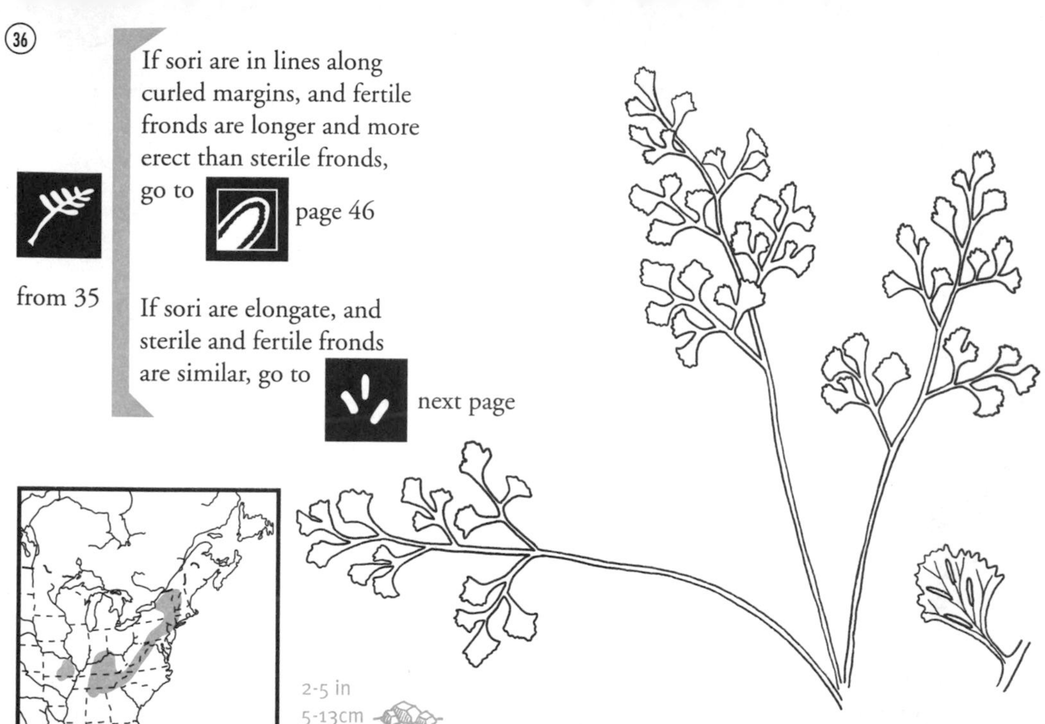

If sori are in lines along curled margins, and fertile fronds are longer and more erect than sterile fronds, go to page 46

from 35

If sori are elongate, and sterile and fertile fronds are similar, go to next page

2-5 in
5-13cm

from 28

If sporangia are on the backs of green, leafy pinnae, go to  page 42

If sporangia are massed on pinnae lacking green, leafy tissue, go to 

If fertile pinnae are at frond tip, and sterile pinnae and pinnules are widely spaced, it is **Royal Fern**
*Osmunda regalis*

If not, go to  next page

2-5 ft
60-150cm

If blade is less than 7 inches (17.5cm) long, go to  page 48

It it's longer, go to 

If blade is delicate and broadest at the middle, and sori are round, it is **New York Fern**
*Thelypteris noveboracensis*

If blade is coarse and broadest above the middle, and fertile frond is smaller than sterile frond and very stiff and woody, it is **Ostrich Fern**
*Matteuccia struthiopteris*

1-2 ft
30-60cm

2-5 ft
60-150cm

from 28

If stipe and rachis are heavily scaled, go to

If stipe is sparsely scaled or scaleless go to

next page

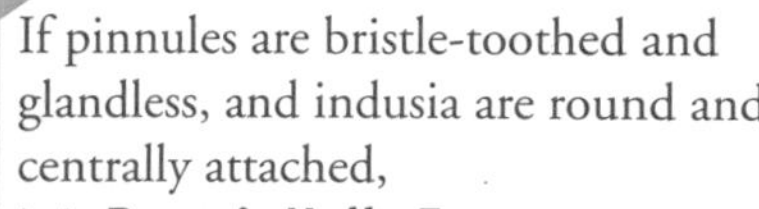

If pinnules are bristle-toothed and glandless, and indusia are round and centrally attached,
it is **Braun's Holly Fern**
*Polystichum braunii*

If pinnules are not bristle-toothed and have minute, aromatic glands, and indusia are kidney-shaped, large, and scale-like, it is **Fragrant Wood Fern**
*Dryopteris fragrans*

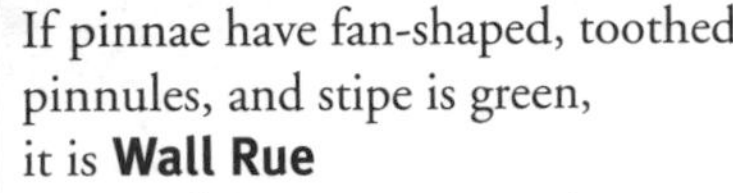

If pinnae have fan-shaped, toothed pinnules, and stipe is green, it is **Wall Rue**

*Asplenium ruta-muraria*

(see page 36)

If pinnae have lobed pinnules, and lower stipe is brown, it is **Mountain Spleenwort**

*A. montanum*

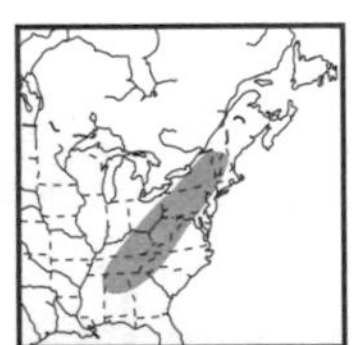

If separate fertile stalk turns cinnamon color and collapses in early summer, and a small, woolly tuft lies at base of each sterile pinna, it is **Cinnamon Fern**

*Osmunda cinnamomea*

If fertile pinnae are in middle of green frond, and sterile pinnae bases lack woolly tufts, it is **Interrupted Fern**

*O. claytoniana*

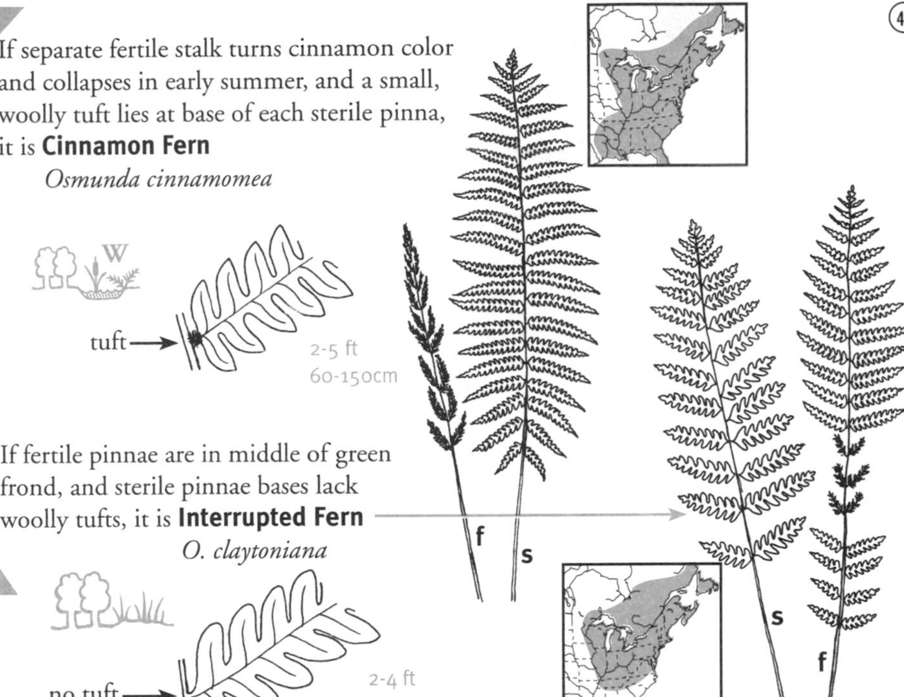

from 40

If sori are funnel-shaped with a black bristle, stipe and rachis are winged, and blade is translucent, it is **Appalachian Filmy Fern**
*Trichomanes boschianum*

If frond lacks this combination of characteristics, go to 

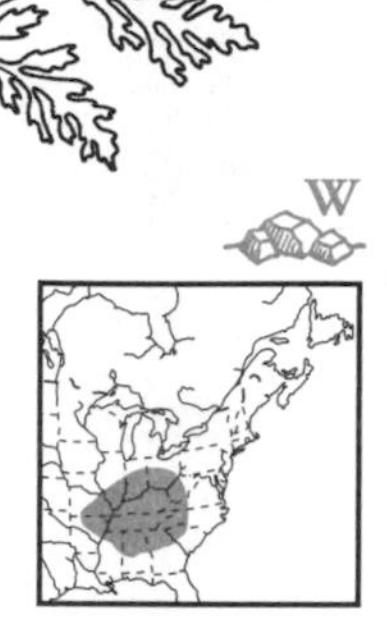


2-6 in
5-15cm

If sori are elongate or hooked, like this: 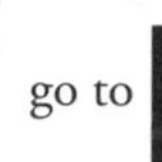 go to  next page

If sori are round, like this:     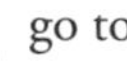 go to  page 47

Look carefully—mature marsh fern sori sometimes look continuous along curled margins, but are round

If sori are indistinct, forming a continuous linear mass along the margin, like this:  go to  page 46

If sori are in broken chains parallel to pinna and pinnule midveins, and fronds are scattered, it is **Virginia Chain Fern**
*Woodwardia virginica*

veining

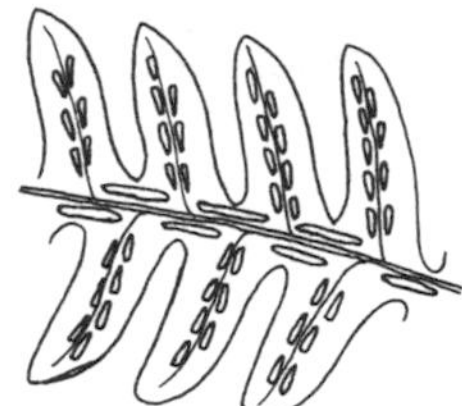

If sori are oblique, and fronds are clustered, go to

next page

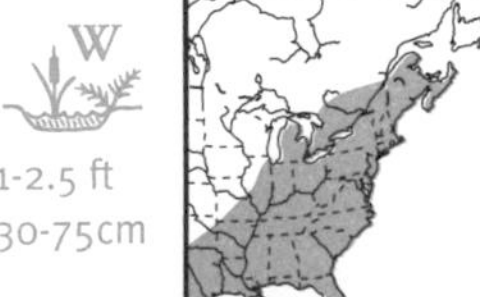

from 43

If frond is more than 12 inches (30.5cm) tall, go to  next page

If it's less than 10 inches (25 cm), and plant grows in rock crevices, go to 

If whole rachis is green and flattened, it is **Mountain Spleenwort**
*Asplenium montanum*

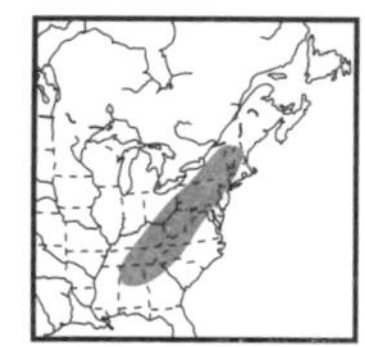

4-8 in
10-20cm

If lower part of rachis is dark, it is **Bradley's Spleenwort**
*A. bradleyi*

If pinnules are cut to midvein of pinnae and deeply toothed, sori are hook-shaped or elongate, and lower stipe has scales, it is **Lady Fern**

*Athyrium filix-femina*

If pinnules are not cut to the midvein and are finely toothed, sori are straight, and stipe has narrow scales and hairs, it is **Silvery Glade Fern**

*Deparia acrostichoides (A. thelypterioides)*

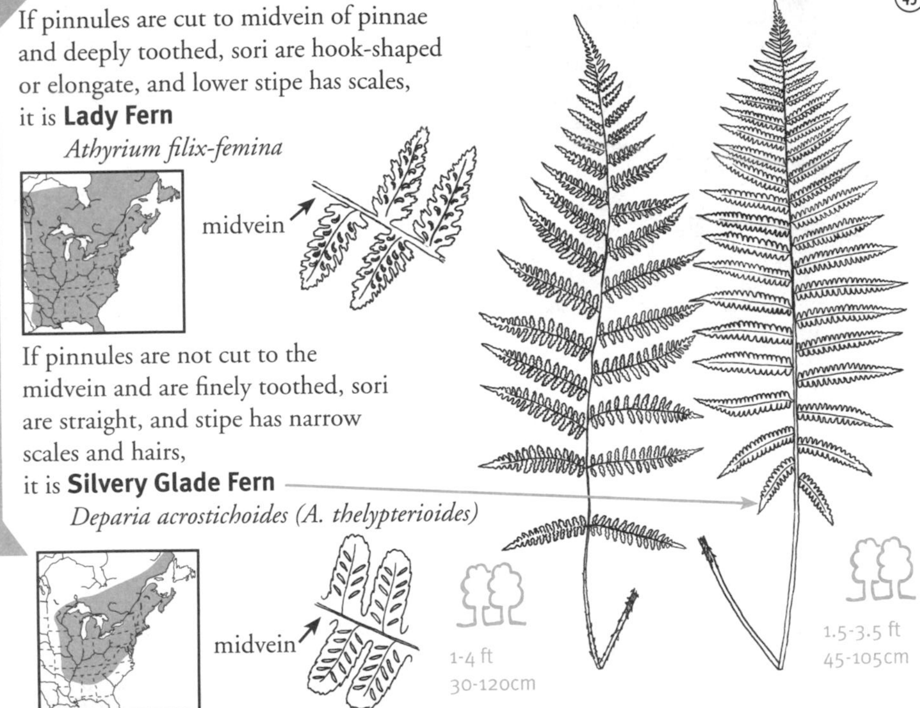

from
36/42

If fronds are densely clustered,
and blades are thick-textured,
it is **Parsley Fern**

*Cryptogramma acrostichoides*

3-6 in
7.5-15cm

If fronds are scattered,
and blades are thin,
fragile, and papery,
it is **Slender Cliffbrake**

*C. stelleri*

3-6 in
7.5-15cm

f
s
f
s

from 42

If frond is less than 9 inches (23cm) long and less than 2 inches (5cm) wide, go to 

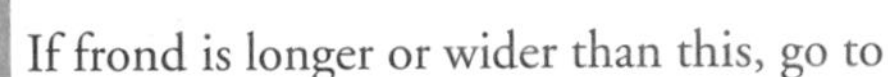

If frond is longer or wider than this, go to  page 50

If stipe is jointed near its base, and blade is not glandular, go to  next page

If stipe is not jointed, and blade is glandular, go to  page 49

If stipe and underside of the blade have dense, rusty hairs, it is **Rusty Woodsia**
*Woodsia ilvensis*

from 39/47

If stipe is yellow-green and frond is smooth, it is **Smooth Woodsia**
*W. glabella*

If stipe is brown and smooth except for a few scales at the base, it is **Alpine Woodsia**
*W. alpina*

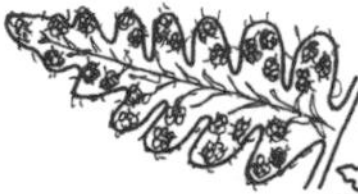

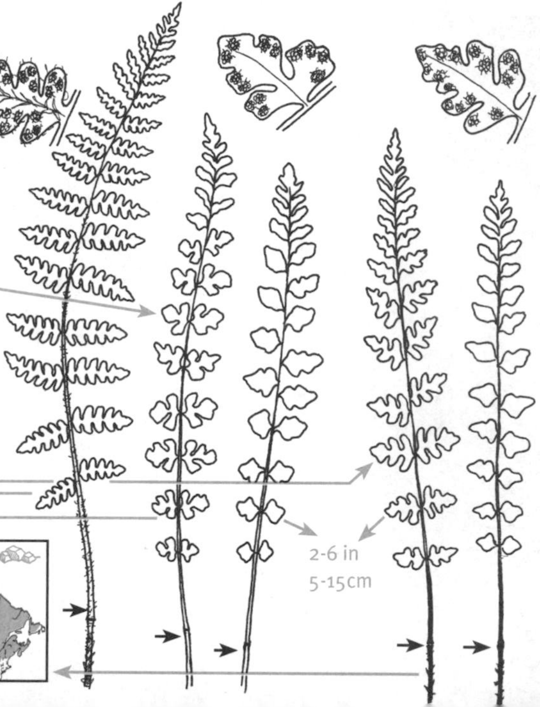

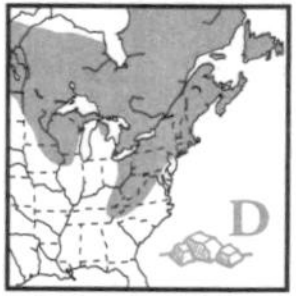

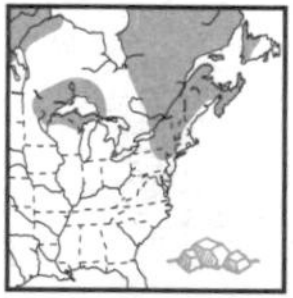

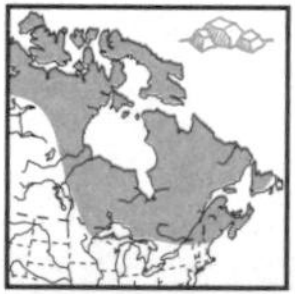

from 47

If frond is fuzzy with whitish hairs, it is **Rocky Mountain Woodsia**
*Woodsia scopulina*

If frond has inconspicuous, minute hairs, and stipe and rachis have narrow scales, it is **Blunt-lobed Woodsia**
*W. obtusa*

If frond lacks hairs and scales, it is **Oregon Woodsia**
*W. oregana*

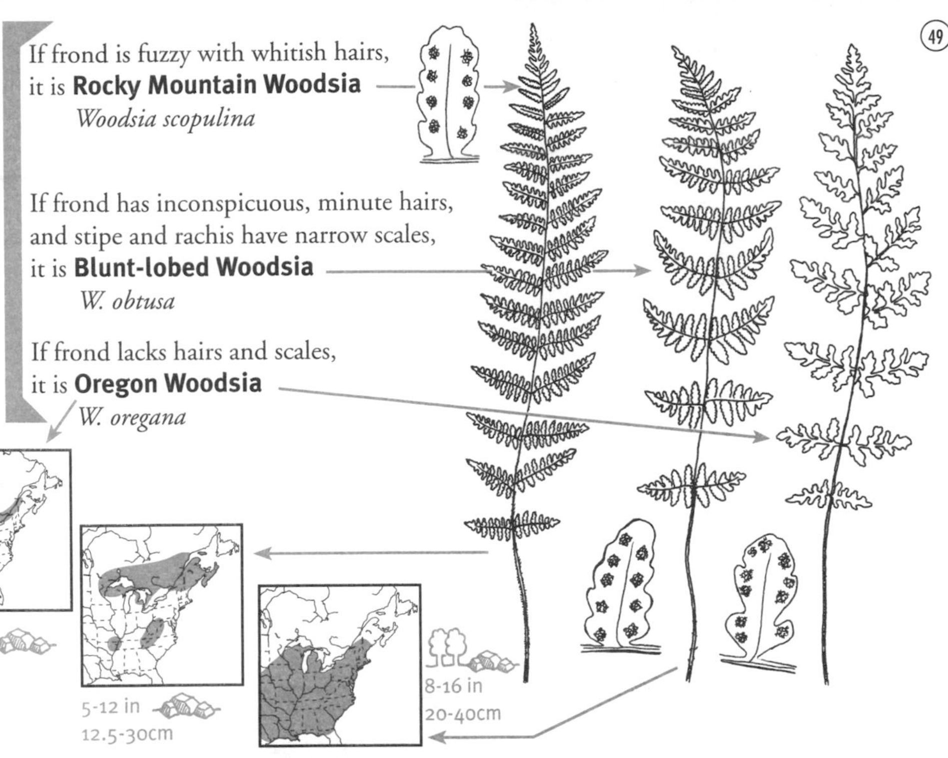

If fronds are clustered, go to  page 52

from 47

If fronds are scattered, go to 

If frond is lacy, has gland-tipped hairs, and is aromatic, and indusium is cup-like, it is **Hay-scented Fern**

*Dennstaedtia punctilobula*

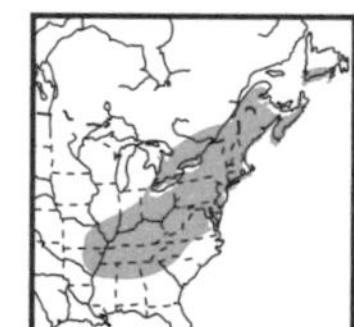


If frond is twice-divided and lacks gland-tipped hairs, go to  next page

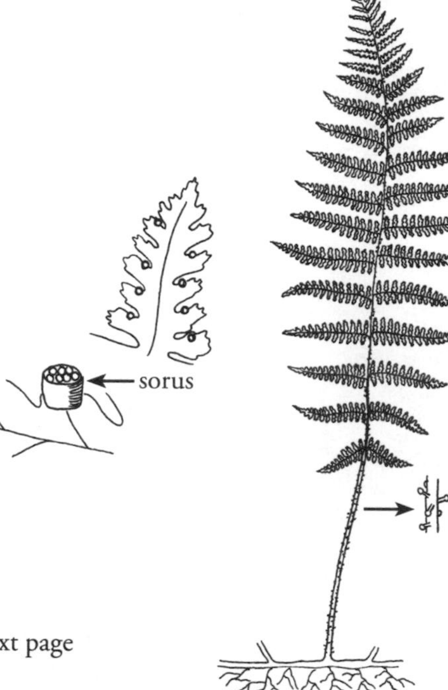

2

If pinnae taper to the rachis
with lowest pair pointing downward,
like this:

and veins are not forked,
it is **Massachusetts Fern**
*Thelypteris simulata*

If pinnae are wide at the
rachis, like this:

and veins are forked,
it is **Marsh Fern**
*T. palustris*

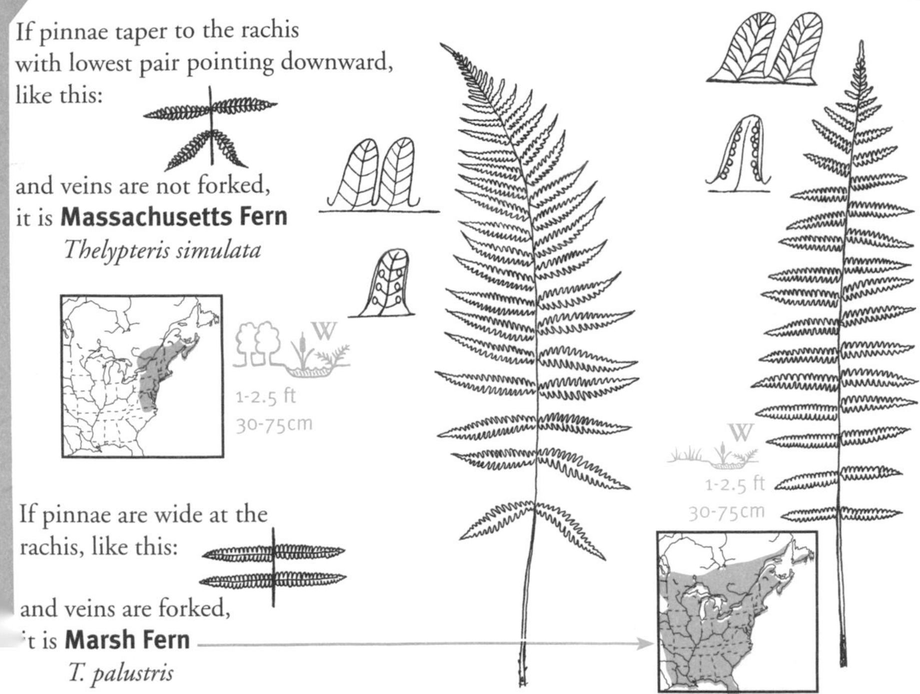

from 50

If stipe has scales or hairs, go to

If stipe lacks scales or hairs (except for sparse scales in early spring) and frond is delicate, it is **Fragile Fern**

*Cystopteris fragilis*

6-15 in
15-38cm

Similar species *C. protrusa* and *C. tenuis*, also called fragile fern, overlap range of *C. fragilis* and extend farther south.

If stipe has large, papery scales, often dense, go to

page 54

If stipe has hairs or small, slender scales, usually sparse, go to

next page

If frond is fuzzy with whitish hairs, and lower pinnae are narrow triangles, it is **Rocky Mountain Woodsia**
*Woodsia scopulina*

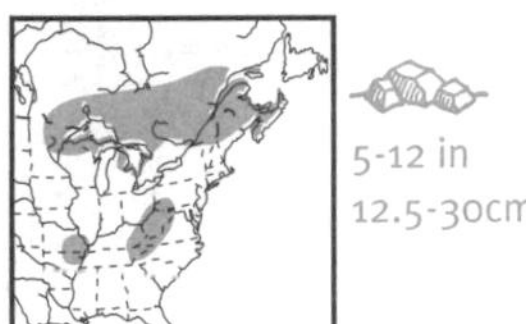

5-12 in
12.5-30cm

8-16 in
20-40cm

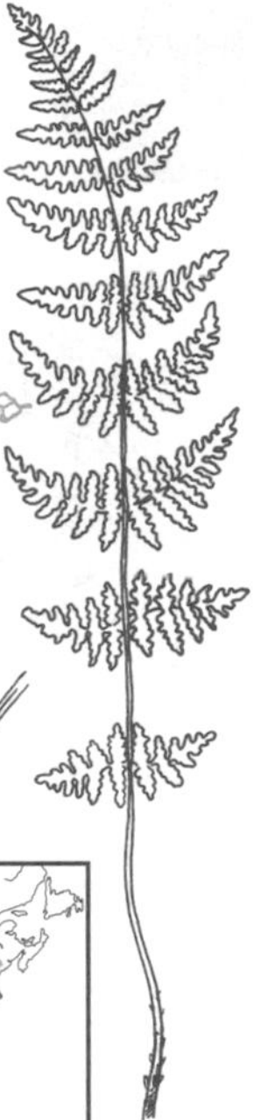

If frond has inconspicuous, minute hairs, and stipe and rachis have narrow scales, and lower pinnae are blunt, broad-lobed triangles, it is **Blunt-lobed Woodsia**
*W. obtusa*

from 52

If sori are marginal,
it is **Marginal Wood Fern**
*Dryopteris marginalis*

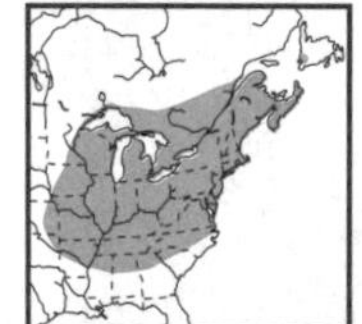

1-2 ft
30-60cm

If not, go to 

Note: Wood Ferns often hybridize, creating confusing forms.

If pinnules have lobes and frond appears lacy, go to  next page

If pinnules have no lobes, go to  page 58

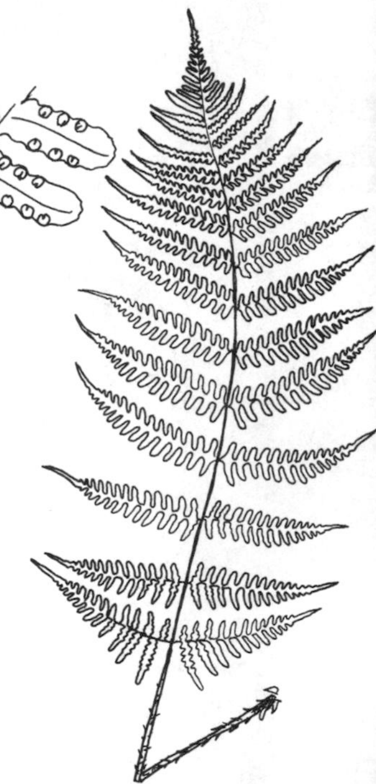

If, on basal pinnae, the first two or three lower pinnules are longer than those directly above, like this:

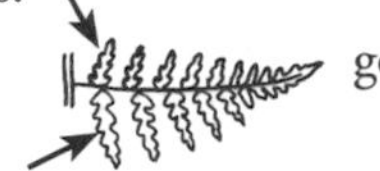

go to

next page

If lower pinnules are equal to those directly above, and stipe is one-fourth as long as rachis, it is **Alpine Lady Fern**

*Athyrium alpestre*

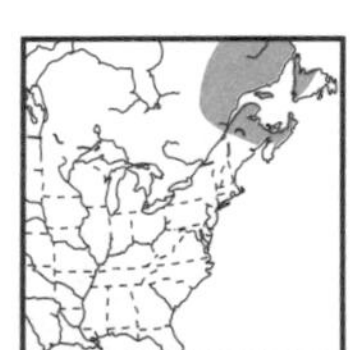

1-2.5 ft
30-75cm

from 55

If fertile frond is taller, more erect, with pinnae more widely spaced on the rachis than sterile frond,
it is **Boott's Wood Fern**
*Dryopteris boottii*

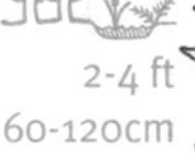

2-4 ft
60-120cm

If fertile and sterile fronds are similar, go to

If, on a basal pinna, the first lower pinnule is shorter than the second, like this:

it is **Evergreen Wood Fern**
*D. intermedia*

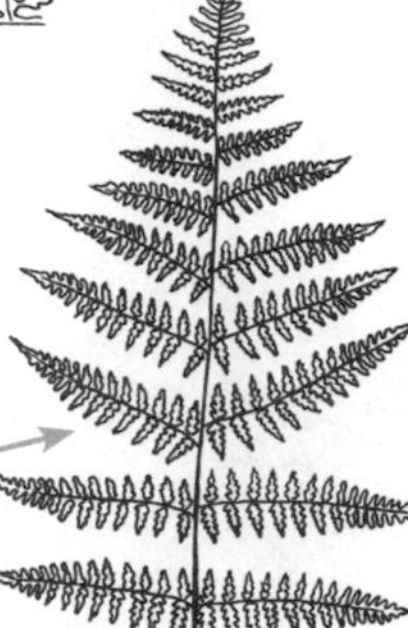

If first lower pinnule is longer than the second, like this:

go to next page

1.5-3 ft
45-90cm

If, on a basal pinna, first lower pinnule is attached almost opposite first upper pinnule, like this:

it is **Spinulose Wood Fern**
*Dryopteris carthusiana*
*(D. spinulosa)*

If first lower pinnule is attached at least midway between first and second upper pinnules, like this:

it is **Spreading Wood Fern**
*D. campyloptera*

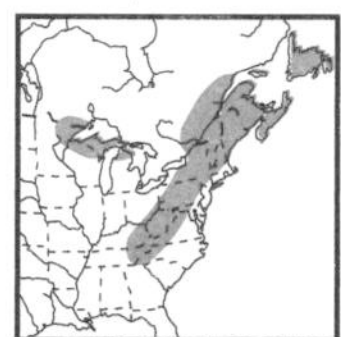

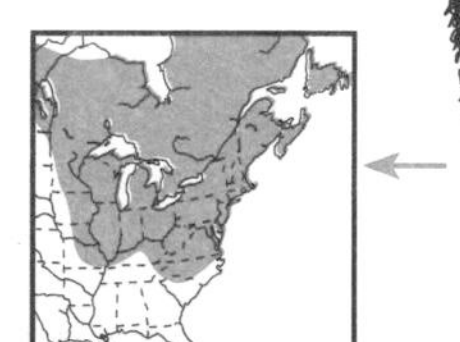

1.5-3 ft
45-90cm

2-3.5 ft
60-105cm

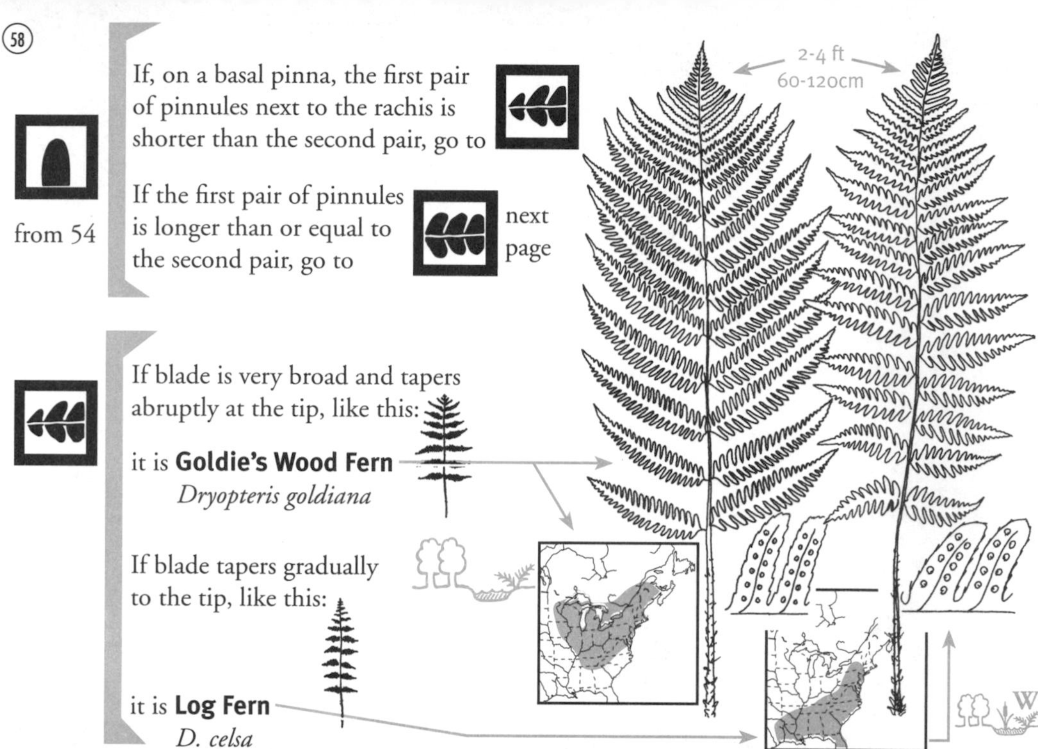

from 54
If, on a basal pinna, the first pair of pinnules next to the rachis is shorter than the second pair, go to
If the first pair of pinnules is longer than or equal to the second pair, go to
next page
If blade is very broad and tapers abruptly at the tip, like this:
it is **Goldie's Wood Fern**
*Dryopteris goldiana*
If blade tapers gradually to the tip, like this:
it is **Log Fern**
*D. celsa*
2-4 ft
60-120cm
W

If pinnae are long and narrow with blunt pinnules, and stipe and rachis are densely scaly, it is **Male Fern**
*Dryopteris filix-mas*

1.5-3.5 ft
45-105cm

If basal pinnae are broadly triangular, go to 

If fertile frond is taller and more erect than sterile frond, and pinnae are twisted at angles to the plane of the blade, it is **Crested Wood Fern**
*Dryopteris cristata*

If fertile and sterile fronds are similar and pinnae are not twisted, it is **Clinton's Wood Fern**
*Dryopteris clintoniana*

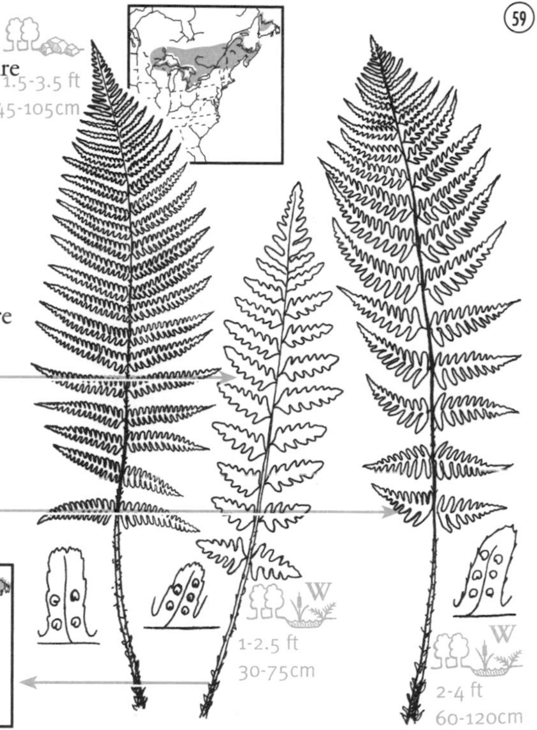

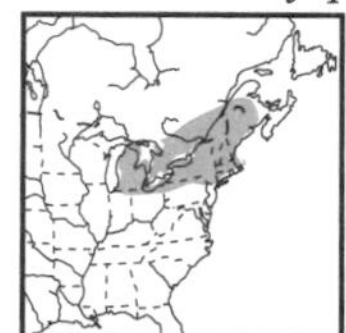

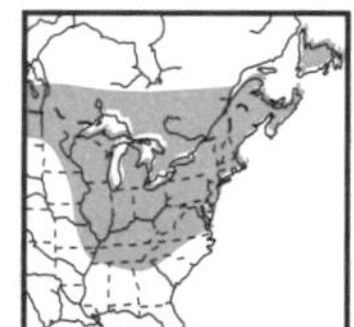

1-2.5 ft
30-75cm

2-4 ft
60-120cm

Other books in the pocket-sized "finder" series:

**for U.S. and Canada east of the Rockies**

- **TREE FINDER** - native and common introduced trees
- **FLOWER FINDER** - spring wildflowers & flower families
- **WINTER TREE FINDER** - leafless winter trees
- **FERN FINDER** - native ferns of the Midwest and Northeast
- **TRACK FINDER** - tracks and footprints of mammals
- **LIFE ON INTERTIDAL ROCKS** - organisms of North Atlantic coast
- **WINTER WEED FINDER** - dry plant structures in winter

**for the Pacific Coast**

- **PACIFIC COAST TREE FINDER** - native trees, Sitka to San Diego
- **REDWOOD REGION FLOWER FINDER** - wildflowers of the coastal fog belt
- **PACIFIC COAST MAMMALS** - mammals, their tracks, other signs

**for Rocky Mtn. and desert states**

- **ROCKY MOUNTAIN TREE FINDER** - native Rocky Mountain trees
- **ROCKY MOUNTAIN FLOWER FINDER** - wildflowers below tree line
- **MOUNTAIN STATE MAMMALS** - mammals, their tracks, skulls, and scat

**for Stargazers**

- **CONSTELLATION FINDER** - patterns in the night sky and star stories

**NATURE STUDY GUIDES are published by KEEN COMMUNICATIONS, PO Box 43673, Birmingham, AL 35243 (888) 604-4537, naturestudy.com. SEE keencommunication.com for our full line of outdoor activity guides by MENASHA RIDGE PRESS and WILDERNESS PRESS. Including regional and national parks hiking, camping, backpacking, and more.**